7/05

The Louisiana Purchase

Christy Steele

WORLD ALMANAC® LIBRARY

Please visit our web site at: www.worldalmanaclibrary.com
For a free color catalog describing World Almanac® Library's list of high-quality books and multimedia programs, call 1-800-848-2928 (USA) or 1-800-387-3178 (Canada). World Almanac® Library's fax: (414) 332-3567.

Library of Congress Cataloging-in-Publication Data

Steele, Christy, 1970-
    The Louisiana Purchase / by Christy Steele.
        p. cm. — (America's westward expansion)
    Includes bibliographical references and index.
    ISBN 0-8368-5789-5 (lib. bdg.)
    ISBN 0-8368-5796-8 (softcover)
    1. Louisiana Purchase—Juvenile literature.   I. Title.
    E333.S74   2005
    973.4'6—dc22   2004056773

First published in 2005 by
World Almanac® Library
330 West Olive Street, Suite 100
Milwaukee, WI 53212 USA

Produced by: EMC—The Education Matters Company
Editors: Christy Steele, Rachael Taaffe
Designer and page production: Jennifer Pfeiffer
Maps and diagrams: Jennifer Pfeiffer
World Almanac® Library editorial direction: Mark J. Sachner
World Almanac® Library art direction: Tammy West
World Almanac® Library production: Jessica Morris
World Almanac® Library editors: Monica Rausch, Carol Ryback

Photo credits: Library of Congress: cover, 4, 6, 7, 10, 11, 12, 15, 16, 17, 18, 21, 22, 24, 28, 30, 31, 35, 37, 40, 43; National Archives: 25, 27, 34; North Wind Picture Archives: 38.

Printed in Canada

1 2 3 4 5 6 7 8 9 09 08 07 06 05

Contents

Chapter 1

The Louisiana Territory

The United States in 1783 was a relatively small country of thirteen states located along North America's East Coast. At this time, possibilities for U.S. expansion were limited by European powers, such as France, Britain, and Spain, that had claimed and established colonies in most of the remaining North American continent.

A main turning point for the United States happened in 1803 with the Louisiana Purchase. In one of the greatest real-estate deals of all time, the United States bought a huge area of land in North America from France. Instantly, the size of the United States almost doubled, and the country quickly entered a period of westward expansion, which is generally regarded as lasting from 1803 until about 1912.

At the time of the sale, Native Americans were living in the territory

◀ Artist Henry Robinson created this portrait of President Thomas Jefferson, who masterminded the Louisiana Purchase at some point between 1840 and 1851.

of the Louisiana Purchase and had been there for thousands of years. Although France had claimed it, the territory had remained largely unexplored by Europeans. President Thomas Jefferson sent explorers to map it, and soon thousands of non-Native settlers moved onto American Indian land.

The settlers were driven by a belief in Manifest Destiny. Writer John O'Sullivan first used this term in 1845 to assert the God-given right of Americans to take over North America and spread U.S. ideas and government to new peoples and territories along the way. To achieve Manifest Destiny, the United States purchased land from other countries and purchased outright or took land from Native peoples until its borders stretched from coast to coast. The Louisiana Purchase was the important first step in this process of westward expansion.

Founding of the Louisiana Territory

In the 1600s, long before the Louisiana Purchase was even considered, European powers dominated the North American continent. Spain controlled present-day Mexico, Florida, and the Southwest, and Great Britain had colonies in Canada and along the East Coast. The French colonized parts of what is now Canada.

In 1682, French explorer René Robert Cavelier, sieur de La Salle, ventured from French Canada on an expedition that led to the Mississippi River Valley. He claimed all the area he explored for France and named it Louisiana, after French King Louis XIV. French fur traders traveled inland from the region's rivers— trapping animals, trading with Native Americans, and building trading posts. The traders added to French land claims until the fan-shaped Louisiana Territory stretched from Canada south to the Gulf of Mexico and from the Appalachian Mountains west

▶ Hernando de Soto, shown here on horseback in this 1876 illustration, became the first documented European to see the Mississippi River in May 1541. De Soto and his men explored much of the land around Louisiana, including parts of what are now Florida, Georgia, and Alabama.

to the Rocky Mountains. It was such a large area that its specific borders were unknown.

The Louisiana Territory's location made it highly desirable to European powers. The country that controlled the territory controlled the mouth of the Mississippi River and the Gulf-Coast region, which contained essential ports for transporting goods. The ruling government could potentially earn large profits by charging duties, or payments, for all shipments entering and leaving the ports.

France's King Louis XIV realized the strategic importance of the Louisiana Territory, and in 1698, he ordered that colonies be started there to protect it from other countries. Frenchmen Pierre Le Moyne, sieur d'Iberville, and Jean-Baptiste Le Moyne, sieur d'Bienville, established several settlements along the Gulf Coast, including New Orleans in 1718. New Orleans proved to be a valuable port near the mouth of the Mississippi River, and it quickly grew to become the largest settlement. French settlers in the region made New Orleans the territory's capital in 1722.

The southern, more populated area of the Louisiana Territory became known as Lower Louisiana.

Meanwhile, Native Americans continued to occupy the northern region, and most continued to live their traditional lifestyles. Some fur traders ventured into the northern region to trade, but it remained largely unsettled by Europeans.

French and Indian War

By 1754, the French controlled land both north (present-day Canada) and far west (the Louisiana Territory) of Britain's colonies on the East Coast. France and Britain, however, disputed ownership of the Ohio River Valley. The Ohio River begins in what is now Pittsburgh, Pennsylvania, and flows to present-day Cairo, Illinois. When the British colonies attempted to expand into the Ohio River Valley region, the dispute led to the French and Indian War (1754–1763).

In this war, the French allied with Spain and Native American groups and fought the British colonists. By 1762, the war was going badly for the French, so they gave the Louisiana Territory to Spain to keep the colony from falling under British control. The Spanish King Carlos III wanted Louisiana as a buffer colony between British colonies and Spain's Mexican gold and silver mines. In 1763, the British won the war, ending France's North American empire and gaining control of Canada.

▼ The first building that housed Louisiana's government, the Spanish Cabildo, was known as the "casa capitular." After the casa capitular burned down in 1788, the Spanish replaced it with this building, completed in 1799. The building became known as the Cabildo when the United States took over Louisiana.

Spanish-Controlled Louisiana

Soon after the war, in 1769, Spain sent soldiers and government representatives to New Orleans to assume control of its new territory. At first, Spain

7

People of Lower Louisiana

About thirty-five thousand people from a variety of ethnic groups lived in Lower Louisiana by 1803. The descendants of the original French settlers were called Creoles and maintained their French culture and language. More French-speaking settlers from Acadia arrived in New Orleans after the British began expelling them from Canada during the French and Indian War.

When Spain assumed control of Louisiana, Spanish settlers from Mexico, the Canary Islands, and Málaga (a province of Spain) settled in St. Bernard and New Iberia. Soldiers and government officials took control and staffed military forts in New Orleans. Descendants of Spanish colonists were often called Creoles, too.

Lower Louisiana was also home to many African slaves from the Senegambia region of Africa's west coast. The region's large population of freed slaves, known then as "free people of color," enjoyed broad rights, including ownership of land and businesses.

About seventy thousand Native Americans, such as the Chitimacha, Houma, and Natchez, lived in the lower Mississippi Valley. Many of them traded with French and Spanish settlers.

limited Louisiana's trade to other Spanish-owned colonies. Since New Orleans and other nearby settlements relied on imported goods to survive, trade limits made life difficult for colonists. Spanish ships did not visit with enough regularity to supply all the colonists' needs. Many Louisiana residents illegally traded with pirates or smugglers to obtain supplies.

To discourage smuggling, the king relaxed trade rules. By the mid-1770s, New Orleans was a busy trading town and an international port. People from around the world sailed to New Orleans to trade goods. Large farms around the city began growing tobacco, indigo, rice, and sugar to export. People brought manufactured goods, lumber, and hides to the city to trade.

San Lorenzo Treaty

In 1783, after the British colonies won independence and formed the United States, thousands of Anglo settlers began crossing the Appalachian Mountains to move to the West. Between 1790 and 1800, the population in what is now Kentucky and Tennessee increased about 300 percent.

Spain disapproved of the Americans moving into its territory and wanted to keep them far from its silver mines. To discourage new settlement, Spanish authorities closed the Mississippi River and the New Orleans port to foreigners, including Americans, in 1784.

The closing of the Mississippi angered many Americans. It caused severe financial hardship to farmers who used the Mississippi to transport their goods. Moving products over land to the East Coast to ship was dangerous, time-consuming, and expensive for western farmers. Many New Englanders, however, were happy with the turn of events. With the river closed, people had to rely on New Englanders for transporting goods along the Atlantic seaboard.

Some in the U.S. government felt that people on the western side of the mountains might not be as loyal to the United States. They worried that those in the west would try to separate and form a new country with its own trading treaty with Spain.

In the 1795 Treaty of San Lorenzo, Spain agreed to open the Mississippi to Americans and allow them the right of deposit, which meant that Americans could unload their goods at Spanish ports without paying fees to the Spanish government. The treaty also set clear borders between Spain and the United States. The United States was given all land east of the Mississippi, and the U.S. southern boundary was set above present-day Florida, which still belonged to Spain.

Napoleon's Plan

World events that began with the French Revolution (1789–1799) changed the destiny of the United States. Until 1789, a king and an aristocratic class ruled France, but on July 14, 1789, French citizens demanding freedom stormed the Bastille, a prison that was the symbol of royal power. In the following months, they overthrew the government and killed the king and many aristocrats by beheading them with guillotines. In 1792, French citizens formed the new French Republic.

Other European countries ruled by monarchies, such as Britain, Prussia, Spain, and the Netherlands, disapproved of the bloody new French Republic. They massed troops and joined together in the War of the First Coalition (1792–1797) to fight French troops and restore the monarchy in

◄ This 1848 illustration shows citizens burning the royal family's luxury carriages during the French Revolution.

France. They failed in their attempt, largely due to the military genius of General Napoleon Bonaparte, a warrior hero of France. He assumed control of France in 1799. In 1801, Bonaparte signed the Treaty of Amiens, a peace agreement with Britain, which ended European fighting for a brief time.

Napoleon Regains Louisiana Territory

Napoleon's great military successes made him want to expand French territory. He decided to build a French empire in North America by regaining the Louisiana Territory from Spain.

Spain's only use for the Louisiana Territory was to separate the United States from its valuable mines. Each year, since Spain did not encourage the development of ports and foreign trading, the colony made little money, and Spain was forced to pay for soldiers to guard strategic locations, such as border areas and forts. King Carlos IV of Spain was eager to part with Louisiana as long as France guaranteed to keep the Americans away from its mines.

In 1800, Spanish and French representatives signed the Treaty of San Idelfonso. In it, Spain gave Louisiana back to France. In return, France guaranteed that it would not give Louisiana to Britain or the United States. Also in this treaty, Napoleon promised to give the Kingdom of Etruria, located in present-day Tuscany, Italy, to King Carlos IV.

▼ This illustration based on a famous 1801 painting shows Napoleon crossing the Alps in 1800 to lead French troops into battle.

Napoleon and King Carlos kept the treaty secret because they did not want the British or Americans to know about the transfer of power. Napoleon worried that the news might cause a war before he was prepared to fight it, because he knew that both Britain and the United States wanted to gain control of the area in order to freely use the Mississippi River.

Saint-Domingue

In addition to the Louisiana Territory, a French colony on the Caribbean island of Hispaniola was crucial to Napoleon's plan for France's empire in North America. In 1697, France gained control of the western third of Hispaniola and founded a colony

▶ Toussaint L'Ouverture, shown on the right, allies himself with the French. L'Ouverture's early education, including reading about the Roman emperor Caesar, helped him become a skillful leader.

it called Saint-Domingue. Spain controlled the rest of the island—a colony named Santo Domingo.

In 1791, inspired by the principles of freedom in the French Revolution, slaves in Saint-Domingue began to revolt. One of the leaders of the rebellion was former slave Toussaint L'Ouverture. Most European plantation owners fled the island, many of them to New Orleans.

Spain believed that the French slave revolt in 1791 offered a perfect opportunity to invade Saint-Domingue and seize control of the entire island. They allied with the British and created a coalition force, which attacked the French colony.

The French knew that they would lose control of their colony if they did not win the revolting slaves back to their side. In 1794, slavery was abolished in all French territories. To gain the slaves' loyalty, French leaders promised to also

Toussaint L'Ouverture (1743–1803)

Toussaint L'Ouverture was born in 1743 in Hispaniola as the eldest son of Gaou-Guinou, a slave from West Africa. Count de Breda owned L'Ouverture's family, but he allowed them to learn to read and write.

When L'Ouverture was young, he worked as a shepherd, and his father taught him the art of using herbs to heal. As an adult, he served as steward over the plantation's sugar-making equipment. Count de Breda gave L'Ouverture freedom when he was about thirty-three. He supported himself by growing coffee.

In 1791, L'Ouverture joined the slaves in their revolt against slaveholders. His military skill made him rise quickly in rank, and soon he was a powerful leader, nicknamed "the Napoleon of the Caribbean." After the French promised freedom to slaves in 1794, L'Ouverture joined their army to fight and encouraged other former slaves to enlist, too. In 1796, L'Ouverture became the directory chief of the army.

In 1800, after winning the war, L'Ouverture expelled the French and helped form the new nation of Haiti. His life was cut short by French plans to regain Haiti. L'Ouverture was captured by the French in 1802 and died in prison in 1803.

grant freedom to them, provided they helped fight against the British and Spanish coalition. Many slaves, encouraged by Toussaint L'Ouverture, began fighting for the French army, and with their help, the French defeated the coalition. In 1796, the French governor appointed L'Ouverture as lieutenant governor of Saint-Domingue.

Spain surrendered control of the whole island to the French in 1797, but Toussaint L'Ouverture used his influence to command the Black army and expelled the French from the island by 1800. After this, the former slaves established the island nation now called Haiti. L'Ouverture remained in charge of the new government and gave himself sweeping powers.

Napoleon, however, had different plans for the island. Napoleon's wars cost a lot of money, and the French treasury was depleted. Saint-Domingue, now Haiti, had valuable cash crops, such as sugar, coffee, and indigo plantations that could help finance Napoleon's empire in the Americas. Napoleon planned to use Louisiana to supply the island with goods. He also plotted to further enlarge his treasury by charging large fees to Americans who wanted to use the Mississippi River or its ports for trade.

To regain Haiti for France, in 1801 Napoleon sent about thirty thousand troops under control of his brother-in-law, General Charles Leclerc. The residents of Haiti did not want to return to slavery and fought bravely for their freedom. Napoleon and Leclerc had not expected such resistance.

General Leclerc felt that Haitians would stop fighting if he captured their leader, Toussaint L'Ouverture. He tricked L'Ouverture into attending a meeting by promising peace and claiming that he would not restore slavery to the island. When L'Ouverture arrived to talk, French troops captured him and sent him by boat to prison in Switzerland. As he left,

◀ Toussaint L'Ouverture presents the newly drafted Haitian constitution to the people. Unfortunately, the constitution did not guarantee their freedom but installed L'Ouverture as governor for life with almost absolute power.

L'Ouverture warned, "In overthrowing me, you have cut down in San Domingue only the trunk of the tree of liberty."

The French lies and Toussaint L'Ouverture's capture only made the local population more determined to fight the French. Many French troops fell victim to fighting, but by early 1803, at least twenty-five thousand more, including Leclerc, had died from yellow fever, a tropical disease carried by mosquitoes. The French troops were unable to secure control of the island and asked Napoleon for reinforcements. The Haitian war was proving much more troublesome than Napoleon had planned, costing France thousands of lives and millions of dollars.

Chapter 3

Americans Debate Expansion

Even though the Treaty of San Idelfonso was secret, Americans had heard rumors about Napoleon's plans of a North American empire beginning in the mid-1790s. They had felt comfortable with Spain's rule of the Louisiana Territory because the 1795 San Lorenzo Treaty had guaranteed them shipping rights on the Mississippi River. French control, however, was met with mixed reaction.

Southern and southwestern states, such as Kentucky and Tennessee, wanted to continue U.S. westward expansion and worried that the region's change of ownership to the aggressive French might close the river and threaten the interests of the United States. Most New Englanders, however,

◀ A 1772 map showing the course of the Mississippi River. In 1772, much of the land west of the Mississippi would still have been marked "unknown" on the map.

did not support U.S. expansion. Congressional leader Rufus King summed up their views: "The feeble policy of our disjointed Government will not be able to unite them. For these reasons I have ever been opposed to encouragements of western immigrants—the States situated on the Atlantic are not sufficiently populous, and loosing [sic] our men, is loosing [sic] our greatest Source of Wealth." Political thought at the time agreed with the position that larger countries were doomed to fail because it was too difficult to govern people at great distances.

New Englanders also were not concerned about Mississippi River navigation or the farmers in the south and west. New England states shared similar commercial interests, primarily fishing and shipping privileges. They wanted to secure their power and did not want to admit more southern or western states into the Union, fearing that U.S. western expansion meant New England would lose the majority of votes in Congress.

▲ An 1883 illustration shows the economic heart of life on the lower Mississippi River, with the cotton planation on the left and the steamboat—which would have carried the newly picked cotton to market—on the right.

Thomas Jefferson and Westward Expansion

In 1801, during this uneasy political climate, Thomas Jefferson became the third president of the United States. He was a Southern politician, writer, statesman, and plantation owner.

Jefferson was a member of the Republican party, a party much different from today's Republican party. Republicans of Jefferson's day believed in a weak federal government, strong states' rights, weak army, support for agricultural development, western expansion, and friendly relations with France. The Federal party was the opposing political group. Federalists were mainly New Englanders who believed in a strong federal government, large army, taxes, weak states, support for fishing and shipping rights along the Atlantic Ocean, the halt of westward expansion, and friendly relations with Britain.

▼ Thomas Jefferson loved Monticello, the home he designed, more than any other place in the world, writing, "I am as happy no where else and in no other society, and all my wishes end, where I hope my days will end, at Monticello."

Jefferson, as did his fellow Republicans, also believed that the United States should expand and would do so gradually as its population increased. He wrote, "Our confederacy must be viewed as the nest from which all America, North and South is to be peopled. We should take care not to press too soon on the Spaniards. Those countries cannot be in better hands. My fear is that they are too feeble to hold them till our population can be sufficiently advanced to gain it from them peice by peice [sic]."

Jefferson realized the importance of the Mississippi ports to the future of the United States. When he heard rumors of Napoleon's plan, he decided to try to purchase New Orleans from France. He wrote that, "There is on the globe one single spot, the possessor of which is our natural and habitual enemy. It is New Orleans, through which the produce of three-eighths of our territory must pass to market. . . . France, placing herself in that door, assumes to us the attitude of defiance."

By 1801, many Americans wanted to take New Orleans by force from Spain before France took official possession of it. The situation was about to erupt into fighting. Jefferson wrote, "Every eye in the United States is now fixed on the affairs of Louisiana. Perhaps nothing since the revolutionary war, has produced more uneasy sensations through the body of the nation." Jefferson, however, wanted to avoid war.

Thomas Jefferson (1743–1826)

Thomas Jefferson—a writer, architect, inventor, farmer, and politician—was one of the founding fathers of the United States. Along with directing the Louisiana Purchase, his greatest achievements include authoring the Declaration of Independence and a Virginia statute guaranteeing freedom of religion.

Jefferson was born in Virginia in 1743. He practiced law after graduating from the College of William and Mary. In addition to his law practice, Jefferson owned a Virginia plantation. He owned slaves and used them to work on his plantation.

Jefferson served in the Virginia House of Burgesses (1769–1775), the Continental Congress (1775–1776), and as governor of Virginia (1779–1781). He moved to Paris in 1785 to serve as the U.S. Minister to France, coming back to the United States to be Secretary of State for President George Washington in 1790. In 1796, Jefferson ran for president but lost and acted as vice president for the winning candidate, President John Adams. Four years later, Jefferson became the third president of the United States and served two terms (1801–1809). He died on July 4, 1826.

Livingston's Mission

To avoid war and secure U.S. interests along the Mississippi, President Jefferson sent prominent lawyer Robert Livingston to France in 1801. Livingston's mission was to find out the terms of the secret treaty between France and Spain. If France did own New Orleans and the Florida region, Livingston was to try and purchase them for the United States.

After arriving in France, Livingston met frequently with French foreign affairs minister Charles-Maurice Talleyrand, a corrupt official accustomed to receiving bribes in exchange for his influence with Napoleon. Despite Livingston's tireless attempts to discover the truth, Talleyrand would not even admit that France had received the Louisiana Territory from Spain. Livingston established U.S. interest in a deal and began negotiations for the Louisiana Purchase, but Talleyrand told Livingston that France could not sell what it did not have.

The Mississippi Crisis

On October 16, 1802, the Spanish closed the Mississippi River to Americans and denied them the right of deposit in New Orleans. Without the right of deposit, Americans could not unload their goods to sell there. People in the United States wondered if the French or Spanish were to blame for the closing as rumors of an approaching French army spread through the West. Spain began turning away American boats laden with goods to trade, and American farmers worried that boats carrying their fall harvests would meet the same fate. Many Americans felt the closing of the river was a treaty violation and an insult to U.S. honor. They demanded that Jefferson declare war.

Jefferson tried to reassure Americans that the closing of the Mississippi was just the act of an over-eager official and not necessarily authorized by the Spanish king. He quickly wrote to Spain demanding that the Spanish government reopen the river to American trade. U.S. Secretary of State James Madison informed the American envoy to Spain that the anger of Americans was understandable because "the Mississippi is to them every thing. It is the Hudson, the Delaware, the Potomac, and all the navigable rivers of the Atlantic states formed into one stream. The produce exported through that channel last year amounted to $1,622,672 from the Districts of Kentucky and Mississippi, and will probably be fifty per cent more this year."

The Mississippi crisis made Jefferson take additional action to avoid war. He appointed James Monroe as envoy extraordinary to France to help Livingston, and Congress approved $2 million to finance the negotiations. Monroe was further authorized to spend up to $9.3 million to buy New Orleans and Florida. If the French would not sell, Monroe was told to negotiate a treaty that guaranteed U.S. trade rights on the Mississippi and other rivers emptying into the Gulf of Mexico. Jefferson wrote to Monroe that "the future destinies of this republic" depended on his mission.

▲ Shipping along the Mississippi evolved from rafts to steam-powered riverboats by the mid-1800s. Workers are loading goods onto these steamboats in Tennessee for transport along the Mississippi River to New Orleans.

Chapter 4

The Deal

Spain did not want to go to war with the United States, and in March 1803, the king instructed Spanish officials in New Orleans to open the Mississippi River to Americans once again.

By this time, however, Monroe was already on his way to France to help Livingston negotiate. The relationship between France and Britain was about to make the Monroe and Livingston's task much easier.

France and Britain

France's relations with Britain were worsening in 1803. Neither country had honored the agreements of the Treaty of Amiens.

Also, with the French defeats in Haiti, Napoleon's dream of a North American empire began to die. He later wrote, "One of the greatest follies I ever was guilty of was sending that army out to St. Domingo." By spring

◀ When relations with Britain soured in 1803, Napoleon abused their ambassador and delivered a tirade at a public reception. English cartoonist James Gillray poked fun at Napoleon's explosive temper with this illustration.

1803, Napoleon had decided to forget Haiti and instead prove French mastery of Europe once and for all. He began planning an invasion of France's main enemy, Britain. Britain, reacting to Napoleon's military actions, sent its warships into the English Channel to protect itself.

Without the income from Saint-Domingue, the Louisiana Territory was not of much use to Napoleon. The war in Haiti had further reduced the French treasury, and he needed money to finance his new war with Britain. Napoleon decided to conveniently ignore his promise to Spain and sell all of Louisiana to the United States to earn income for the war effort. He declared, "I renounce Louisiana. It is not only New Orleans that I will cede, it is the whole colony without any reservation. I know the price of what I abandon. . . . I renounce it with the greatest regret. To attempt obstinately to retain it would be folly."

On April 12, 1803, Napoleon instructed his minister of the treasury, François de Barbé-Marbois, to handle the sale. Napoleon wanted about 50 million francs, which was about $10 million, for the territory, and he wanted the deal made quickly to fund the supplies and troops he needed for war.

The Deal Is Made

Barbé-Marbois and Livingston discussed the possibilities of a sale on April 13. Barbé-Marbois, a clever negotiator, set the price at $25 million dollars, well above Napoleon's asking price.

Livingston was excited that France wanted to sell the huge territory. He conveyed U.S. interest in the land deal but said that the United States would pay only 20 million francs, about $4 million. Barbé-Marbois made a counter offer of $15 million, but nothing was decided that evening because Monroe had to be properly introduced to French officials before beginning formal negotiations. That night, Livingston wrote a letter to James Madison about the turn of events, saying "We shall do all we can to cheapen the purchase, but my present sentiment is we shall buy."

Monroe was officially presented to the French on April 14, and formal negotiations began by April 15. After several weeks of arguing price with Barbé-Marbois, Livingston and Monroe agreed to pay $11,250,000 for the territory and $3,750,000 worth of France's debts to U.S. citizens. This deal made the total cost of the whole territory of Louisiana just $15 million. Although its boundaries were not firmly set, the area was about 828,000 square miles (2,144,510 square kilometers), which meant the United States paid about 4 cents per acre ($1.60 per hectare) for the land.

The Americans and Barbé-Marbois quickly wrote a treaty ceding Louisiana to the United States. Monroe sent a letter to Washington, D.C., describing the deal, but he and Livingston decided to make the purchase without waiting for Congress and President Jefferson's formal authorization. Napoleon could change his mind at any moment, and they could not risk the months-long delay that sending authorization by ship would require.

▲ James Monroe's success with the Louisiana Purchase helped him become the fifth president of the United States (1817–1825). This portrait shows him sometime between 1830 and 1842.

The Louisiana Purchase Treaty

To appease Napoleon, the U.S. ministers left some difficult issues unresolved in the Louisiana Purchase Treaty. One issue in the deal was the unknown boundaries of the territory. When Livingston asked Talleyrand the specific borders, he replied, "I do not know. You must take it as you received it. . . . I can give you no directions. You have made a noble bargain for yourselves, and I suppose you will make the most of it." As a temporary solution, Monroe put into the new treaty the exact wording of the old Treaty of San Idelfonso with Spain that gave the Louisiana Territory to France.

Another issue was that Napoleon and Barbé-Marbois wanted the rights of Louisiana residents protected under the treaty. To complete the sale, Monroe and Livingston were forced to approve an article stating that the United States would offer statehood for Louisiana as soon as possible and give to its residents "all the rights, advantages and immunities of citizens of the United States." This offer went against the wishes of Jefferson and Madison who felt the residents of Louisiana were not ready to govern themselves.

Despite these issues, the Louisiana Purchase Treaty was agreed upon on April 30, but the English translation was not ready to sign until May 5, 1803. On that day, Monroe, Livingston, and Barbé-

▼ The U.S. copy of the Louisiana Purchase Treaty is kept in the National Archives in Washington, D.C. The initials "P.F." on the cover stand for "Peuple Français."

Napoleon Bonaparte (1769–1821)

Napoleon Bonaparte was born on the French-owned island of Corsica in 1769 to Italian parents Carlo and Letizia Buonaparte. In 1779, when he was ten, Napoleon entered military school in France and began to learn French.

When the French Revolution erupted in 1789, Napoleon joined the French revolutionary army and fought against the royalists, or those who supported the monarchy. On November 18, 1799, Napoleon led the military in a government takeover and became First Counsel of France. Napoleon crowned himself emperor of France for life in 1804 and tried to expand France's empire in Europe.

European powers united to fight Napoleon, and he returned to war several times, gaining new territory for France through conquest each time. In 1805, he signed a treaty with the Russian Tsar Alexander I to divide Europe between France and Russia. Napoleon then controlled Germany, Switzerland, and half of Poland. In 1805, he became the King of Italy, and in 1808 he invaded Spain and made his brother Joseph king.

The Spanish, with the help of British troops, revolted against Joseph, and the French were pushed from Spain in 1813. Events in Spain were the beginning of the end for Napoleon. He then attacked his former ally, Alexander I, and invaded Russia in 1812. The invasion proved disastrous, and the Russians were able to defeat French troops in several battles.

Taking advantage of France's weakness, the European countries united and fought against Napoleon. They defeated his forces and forced him into exile on the tiny island of Elba in 1814.

Napoleon, however, escaped from Elba in 1815 and took control of France once again. He was finally defeated at the Battle of Waterloo by European troops and placed in permanent exile on Saint Helena. He died there on May 5, 1821.

Marbois signed the treaty ceding the Louisiana Territory to the United States. Livingston sensed the importance of that moment and said, "We have lived long, but this is the noblest work of our whole lives. . . . From this day the United States take their place among the powers of the first rank."

James Monroe secured funding for the sale from European banks. Napoleon used all the money from the deal to fund his war machine. Several weeks later, Britain and France were fighting once again.

The U.S. ministers had paid much more money and bought more land than Congress had authorized, and they hoped their actions would be approved in the United States.

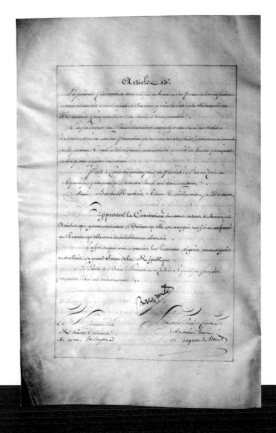

Enjoyment of Their Liberty

The Louisiana Treaty consisted of three documents—the actual treaty and two documents containing articles describing additional terms.

" The Government of the United States engages to pay to the French government in the manner Specified in the following article the sum of Sixty millions of francs independant of the Sum which Shall be fixed by another Convention for the payment of the debts due by France to citizens of the United States."

"The inhabitants of the ceded territory shall be incorporated in the Union of the United States and admitted as soon as possible according to the principles of the federal Constitution to the enjoyment of all these rights, advantages and immunities of citizens of the United States, and in the mean time they shall be maintained and protected in the free enjoyment of their liberty, property and the Religion which they profess. "

Chapter 5

The United States Reacts

The ship carrying the U.S. ministers' letters about the sale reached Washington, D.C., in late June 1803, almost one month after the treaty was signed. The president and the secretary of state were thrilled with the unexpected news. Madison quickly wrote to approve the purchase.

On June 30, 1803, the first newspapers reported the facts of the Louisiana Purchase to Americans. Ships and post riders, riders who traveled by horseback to transport mail and news, quickly carried the story around the United States. Jefferson confirmed the news at Washington, D.C.'s, Independence Day celebration, and newspapers that supported the president heaped praise on him. The *Intelligencer* wrote, "We have secured our rights by pacific means. Truth and reason have been more powerful than the sword."

◀ James Madison, shown in this 1828 portrait, served as the fourth president of the United States (1809–1817).

The Louisiana Purchase

BRITISH TERRITORY

WA
OR
ID
MT
ND
MN
WI
MI
Lake Superior
Lake Huron
Lake Michigan
L. Erie
Ontario
ME
VT
NH
MA
NY
RI
CT
PA
NV
UT
WY
SD
IA
NE
IL
IN
OH
WV
NJ
MD
DE
CA
CO
LOUISIANA TERRITORY
KS
MO
KY
VA
UNITED STATES
NC
TN
Mississippi R.
AZ
NM
OK
AR
MS
AL
GA
SC
TX
FL
NEW SPAIN
Pacific Ocean
Gulf of Mexico
Atlantic Ocean

LEGEND
River
Louisiana Purchase, 1803
Present-day State Borders

200 mi
300 km

Jefferson realized that the purchase, "removes from us the greatest source of danger to our peace." Other leaders agreed, and hundreds of letters of congratulations reached the president at the White House. One wrote that the Louisiana Purchase "has the air of enchantment as the greatest and most beneficial event that has taken place since the Declaration of Independence."

▲ This map shows the approximate boundaries of the Louisiana Purchase.

Federalist Complaints

Not everyone, however, was pleased that the size of the United States had instantly doubled. Some Federalists, fearing loss of political power, were quick to criticize Jefferson. Federalist leader Fisher Ames complained that the purchase was "a great waste, a wilderness unpeopled with any beings except wolves and wandering Indians. . . . We are to give money of which we have too little for land of which we already have too much."

IN THE COTTON FIELD.

▲ 1863 illustration of slaves picking cotton. Abolitionists feared that the Louisiana Purchase would create more slave states. The number of representatives for each state in the House of Representatives depended on population—and each slave in a state was counted as three-fifths of a person, even though they could not vote. This gave their Anglo masters even more power and say in how the United States would be governed.

Those in New England worried that the new states eventually created in the territory of the Louisiana Purchase would be loyal to Jefferson and Virginia. They felt that the Northern states would lose influence in government as these future Southern states would receive two votes each in the Senate.

Abolitionists, people who wanted to outlaw slavery, were also concerned about the purchase. Thomas Jefferson and Southern farmers supported slavery, and abolitionists worried that any new Southern states created from the territory would be pro-slavery. An article in the *Balance and Columbian Repository* asked, "Will republicans . . . purchase an immense wilderness for the purpose of cultivating it with the labor of slaves?"

Some in the United States did not trust the residents of Louisiana to be loyal to their new country. The traditionally European New England states disapproved of the diverse ethnic and racial mix of the population and the clause in the treaty that offered them the rights of citizens. They worried that the new people were too different from Anglo Americans and would forever change the character of the United States. Fisher Ames claimed that "otters" were better able to rule themselves than Louisiana's "savages and adventurers."

Constitutional Issues

Despite the signature of U.S. ministers, the Louisiana Purchase Treaty was not official until Congress ratified, or approved, it. Before asking Congress to ratify the treaty, Thomas Jefferson wanted to pass a Constitutional amendment that specifically allowed the purchase, and he spent seven weeks writing one that divided the territory between Anglos and Native Americans.

Jefferson did this because he believed in a strict interpretation of the Constitution. He felt that acting on implied powers of the Constitution would weaken the document and make it possible for the government to misuse its power. As it was written, the Constitution did not state that land could be purchased and added to the Union. Jefferson, therefore, felt that the Louisiana Purchase was unconstitutional without the passing of an amendment.

The president was forced to abandon the amendment after receiving a letter from Robert Livingston, who was still in Paris. Napoleon had just crowned himself as emperor of France and was now reconsidering the sale. Livingston warned that any delay or debate about the treaty might make Napoleon change his mind about the whole deal.

Jefferson quickly convened Congress. He needed a two-thirds vote to ratify a treaty. The debate in the House of the Representatives was fierce, and many did not support the treaty because of the Constitutional issues. Others claimed that the clauses in the Constitution calling for action that was "necessary and proper" if the action supported the "general welfare" were enough

▼ An 1847 illustration shows Napoleon as emperor of France. Napoleon started out as a revolutionary but eventually seized power for himself as emperor. He explained this move by saying, "I had been nourished by reflecting on liberty, but I thrust it aside when it obstructed my path."

Jefferson's Native American Policy

One of Jefferson's main concerns after the Louisiana Purchase was how to handle the Native Americans who lived on the land. He believed that, to keep Native Americans from attacking Anglo settlers, he had to be sure they feared the U.S. government. He also believed Native Americans should live separate from Anglos to maintain peace.

In 1803, Jefferson drafted a Constitutional amendment to divide the Louisiana Purchase between Anglos and Native Americans. As part of his plan, eastern land that belonged to Indians would be taken away, and they would be moved to new western land in the Louisiana Territory. Jefferson expected the Native Americans would offer little resistance because "our strength and their weakness is now so visible that they must see we have only to shut our hand to crush them."

Although Jefferson's amendment was never introduced to Congress, his ideas were later put into action by President Andrew Jackson. Under Jackson, Congress passed the Indian Removal Act of 1830, and the U.S. Army forced thousands of Native Americans to leave their homelands and move to reservations in the West.

to justify the purchase. In the end, the Republican majority won. In October, both houses of Congress voted to approve the purchase.

Jefferson and Congress, however, chose to ignore the clause that gave rights of citizens to those in the new territory. Jefferson claimed, "They were as yet as incapable of self-government as children." Instead of letting the residents vote and choose their government, Congress wanted to treat the area like a colony. Jefferson appointed a governor and legislative council with almost dictator-like power to govern until those in Congress felt the Louisiana residents were prepared to become citizens.

U.S. Assumes Control of Louisiana Territory

Meanwhile, Spain was voicing disapproval over the sale of Louisiana to the United States because Napoleon had violated their treaty by breaking his promise not to sell. U.S. leaders were worried that Spanish soldiers in the territory would fight to keep it. They were also unsure how the residents of Louisiana would react to having their land sold to another country once again.

France helped ease the transfer of power. On November 30, 1803, Spain gave control of the territory to French Governor Pierre Clément Laussat. Believing that France was now in control, Laussat quickly disbanded the Spanish military and sent them sailing for Spain. In its place, he formed a volunteer fire company and several companies of American and French soldiers. He also changed the style of government from the Spanish Cabildo, or all-Spanish ruling council, to a mayor-and-council system of government that included Frenchmen, Spaniards, and Americans. He also put into place the French Code Noir, a set of policies that more strictly governed slaves and free Blacks than the previous Spanish policies had. Laussat did this all in three weeks and was horribly disappointed when he received word from France that Louisiana had been sold to the United States.

The U.S. government sent General James Wilkinson and about four hundred American troops to ensure that the appointed Louisiana governor, William Claiborne, smoothly assumed U.S. control of New Orleans and Lower Louisiana. Claiborne was a loyal Republican and had previously served as the governor of the Mississippi Territory. Claiborne, however, had no knowledge of French or Spanish, and yet Jefferson expected him to control the diverse population of Louisiana and prepare them for statehood.

On December 20, 1803, troops lowered the French flag and raised the American Stars and Stripes at the Cabildo, New Orleans's military fort. Americans living in New Orleans cheered, but Laussat and other sad Louisiana residents sobbed. Three weeks later, the French gave control of northern Louisiana to the United States in St. Louis.

onfidential.

Gentlemen of the Senate and of
As the continuance of
Indian tribes will be under
sefsion, I think it my duty
in the execution of that act
continuing it, in the present
if that shall, on the whole
The Indian tribes re
-siderable time, been growing
of the territory they occupy,
policy has long been gaining
sale on any conditions. in
and excites dangerous jealo
overture for the purchase of
only are not yet obstinately
counteract this policy of their
rapid increase of our numbe
-ent. First, to encoura
-ing stock, to agriculture a
themselves that lefs land &
their former mode of living.
will then become uselefs, & th
means of improving their far
Secondly to multiply tr
those things which will contr
-on of extensive, but uncu
-lope to them the wisdom of
what we can spare and the

Chapter 6

Corps of Discovery

E ven before the Louisiana Purchase was made, Jefferson's belief in U.S. western expansion had him dreaming of exploring the unknown west. He had tried twice before to send exploring expeditions across the continent but had failed each time.

While Jefferson was president, two-thirds of the American population lived about 50 miles (80 kilometers) from the Atlantic Ocean. By 1803, there were only four paths that crossed the Appalachian Mountains, and only one-half million Americans lived west of the mountain chain. Jefferson wanted to encourage movement westward, but to do that effectively, he needed more information about the western territory. Even before the United States owned it, he began planning an expedition to the West.

◀ President Jefferson sent this secret letter to Congress in January 1803. It asks Congress to fund a western exploring expedition.

Reasons for Expedition

Anglo settlers were fearful of moving too far west because there were too many unknown elements, such as the terrain, the water supply, and the animals. At the time, some writers had described the western land as containing unicorns, huge beavers the size of horses, mountains of salt, and exploding volcanos. Anglos were also unsure of the reception they might receive from the Native Americans who lived there.

Settlers also did not want to be too far from supply routes. Crucial to westward movement was the establishment of new trails and maps, which Jefferson hoped an exploring expedition could create. Maps of the West were often inaccurate and pictured California as an island. Great areas of the maps were blank, and Jefferson wanted these spaces filled.

Jefferson also hoped to find the famed Northwest Passage. Until North America was mapped, many people thought there

▼ Meriwether Lewis and William Clark explored about 8,000 miles (12,875 km) of lands west of the Mississippi River. This map shows their route, as well as the boundaries of the Louisiana Purchase.

was an undiscovered water route called the Northwest Passage that would lead to the Pacific. Such a route would make trade to Asia faster and easier, as well as greatly increase U.S. wealth.

The Mission

On January 18, 1803, Jefferson secretly asked Congress to fund the first U.S. government-sponsored exploration and form a "Corps of Discovery" to explore and map the West. He kept it secret because the western areas were, at the time, owned by Britain, France, and Spain. On February 28, 1803, Congress approved Jefferson's plan and authorized $2,500 to fund the trip.

After the Louisiana Purchase, the mission of the expedition changed, and it no longer had to be secret. Now it was a bold survey of American-owned land in search of trading opportunities and natural resources.

The Corps of Discovery

Jefferson placed his personal secretary, Captain Meriwether Lewis, in charge of the Corps of Discovery. Lewis was known for his military and wilderness skills, including riding, hunting, and hiking. Helping Lewis was his trusted friend and former army companion, William Clark. Once Congress approved the mission, Lewis began several months of scientific instruction Jefferson felt would be useful to him on the journey, including botany, zoology, astronomy, navigation, and mapmaking.

On July 5, 1803, Lewis went to Pittsburgh to purchase supplies for the expedition. The provisions included maps, books, food, cloth for tents, guns, ammunition, pots, eating utensils, fishing hooks and lines, clothing, soap, salt, writing paper and pens, ink, and medical and scientific equipment. The expedition would also need gifts, such as tomahawks, needles, thread, scissors, ribbons, tobacco, and beads, to secure the goodwill of any Native American groups they might meet.

About forty-eight men from around the United States were involved in the expedition, including a carpenter, a tailor, former soldiers, scientists, adventurers, and a slave of Clark's. Many of them spent the winter of 1803–1804 training in Camp Wood, which the Corps built near St. Louis on the east bank of the Mississippi River. Jefferson instructed the explorers to write about the western territory's plants, animals, minerals, peoples and their customs, as well as map the terrain and forge a new trail to the Pacific Ocean.

The Journey

On May 14, 1804, the Corps began their two-and-a-half year journey by sailing up the Missouri River in a special large keelboat built to haul the expedition's supplies and recruits. Additionally, they paddled two smaller boats in case something should happen to the keelboat. On May 25, they passed the last Anglo settlement along the river.

On August 3, the Corps encountered their first group of Native Americans, from the Oto and Missouri tribes. The Corps gave the Indians gifts, including U.S. flags. In an attempt to build alliances with the Native groups, the Corps told them they had a new "great father" in the East who would treat them well if they did not fight the Anglos. On the long journey, the Corps also met with the Lakota Sioux, Mandan, Shoshone, Nez Percé, Clatsops, Blackfeet, and Hidatsa peoples. Most Native Americans were receptive to relations and traded with them. To help them communicate with Native Americans, in

▲ Meriwether Lewis (top) was called "the greatest pathfinder this country has ever known" for his leadership of the expedition. William Clark (bottom), his co-captain, would later serve as Indian agent.

▲ In this painted scene, the Corps is presenting gifts to Native Americans in order to build alliances with Indian groups in the Louisiana Territory.

November 1804, they hired French-Canadian trapper Toussaint Charbonneau, who had traded with many different Indian groups, to serve as interpreter. Charbonneau brought his wife Sacagawea, a Shoshone woman who served as a valuable guide and interpreter for the Corps.

As a winter home during 1804–1805, the Corps built Camp Mandan on the Missouri River across from a large village of Mandans near today's Bismarck, North Dakota. In spring, Lewis sent some men and the keelboat back to Jefferson with sketches and samples of plants and animals they had found.

The Corps's remaining journey took them to places no Anglo had ever seen. They saw the Missouri River's white sandstone cliffs, Great Falls, and headwaters. They were the first Americans known to reach the Continental Divide and cross the Rocky and Bitterroot Mountains—both mountain ranges proved much more extensive than they had thought.

The explorers ran out of provisions in the Bitterroot Mountains and nearly starved before reaching Idaho, where the Nez Percé Indians fed them salmon and taught them how to make canoes from logs. The Corps used the new canoes to navigate the Clearwater, Columbia, and Snake Rivers, finally emerging from the rain forests of the Pacific Northwest to their destination, the Pacific Ocean. For their 1805–1806 winter camp, they built Fort

Clatsop on the Columbia River, near present-day Astoria, Oregon.

The following spring, the Corps turned around and came home. They split into four groups and took different routes in order to explore more of the territory, reuniting in August near the mouth of the Yellowstone River. On September 23, 1806, the explorers arrived back in St. Louis.

In all, the Corps mapped about 4,000 miles (6,436 km). They found and sketched about one hundred twenty-two animals never before heard of by Anglos in the East, including coyotes, prairie dogs, buffalo, grizzly bears, mule deer, and antelope. They also detailed one hundred seventy-eight new plants, including corn.

Lewis and Clark's exploration of the Louisiana Territory captured the imagination of the whole nation and started a flood of western settlement. Guided by maps drawn by Lewis and Clark, people moved West in search of a fresh start and new opportunities.

Most Perfect Harmony

These creatively spelled entries are from the journal of Captain Meriwether Lewis of the Corps of Discovery.

"September 16, 1804
vast herds of Buffaloe deer Elk and Antilopes were seen feeding in every direction as far as the eye of the observer could reach.

April 07, 1805, Fort Mandan
Our vessels consisted of six small canoes, and two large perogues. This little fleet altho' not quite so rispectable as those of Columbus or Capt. Cook, were still viewed by us with as much pleasure as those deservedly famed adventurers ever beheld theirs; and I dare say with quite as much anxiety for their safety and preservation. we were now about to penetrate a country at least two thousand miles in width, on which the foot of civilized man had never trodden; the good or evil it had in store for us was for experiment yet to determine, and these little vessells contained every article by which we were to expect to subsist or defend ourselves. ... enterta[in]ing as I do, the most confident hope of succeeding in a voyage which had formed a da[r]ling project of mine for the last ten years, I could but esteem this moment of my departure as among the most happy of my life. The party are in excellent health and sperits, zealously attached to the enterprise, and anxious to proceed; not a whisper of murmur or discontent to be heard among them, but all act in unison, and with the most perfict harmony.

April 17, 1805
there were three beaver taken this morning by the party. the men prefer the flesh of this anamal, to that of any other which we have, or are able to procure at this moment. I eat very heartily of the beaver myself, and think it excellent; particularly the tale, and liver. **"**

39

Chapter 7

The Legacy of the Louisiana Purchase

Exploration of the new territory excited the nation, but not all effects of the Louisiana Purchase were positive. Its vague borders caused conflict between the United States and Spain. The United States believed their land stretched to the Sabine River, but Spain disagreed. The dispute grew so heated that the two countries broke political contact in 1805.

To prevent a war, in 1806 the two countries appointed a neutral strip of land called the Sabine Free State to serve as a buffer between the two territories. In 1810, James Madison annexed western Florida from Spain. The Sabine Free State ceased to exist in 1819 when Spain sold all of Florida to the United States for $5 million in

◀ New Orleans grew rapidly after the Louisiana Territory became part of the United States. This 1885 illustration shows the growing city and the Mississippi River.

the Adams-Onís Treaty, which also set the boundary between Louisiana and Texas at the Sabine River.

From Territory to Louisiana Statehood

In 1804, Congress reorganized the Louisiana Purchase into two sections. Lower Louisiana—including the city of New Orleans—became the Orleans Territory, and the northern region became the District of Louisiana. The District of Louisiana became an official territory in 1805. Orleans Territory Governor William Claiborne, based in New Orleans,

▼ This map shows the changing borders of the United States.

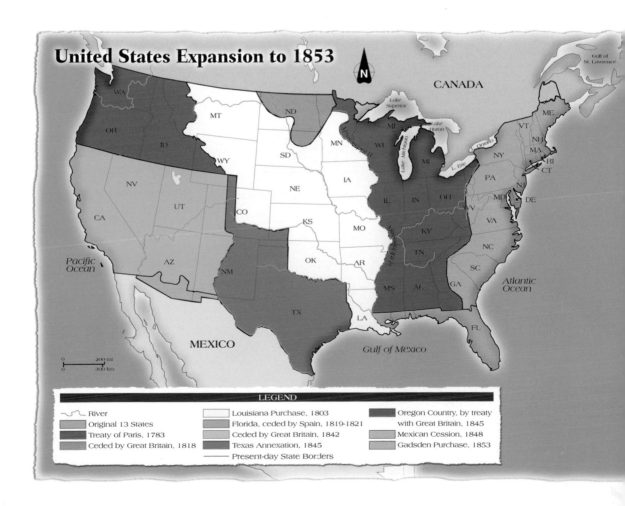

United States Expansion to 1853

LEGEND

~~~ River
Original 13 States
Treaty of Paris, 1783
Ceded by Great Britain, 1818

Louisiana Purchase, 1803
Florida, ceded by Spain, 1819-1821
Ceded by Great Britain, 1842
Texas Annexation, 1845
Present-day State Borders

Oregon Country, by treaty with Great Britain, 1845
Mexican Cession, 1848
Gadsden Purchase, 1853

struggled to make the local government of the Orleans Territory less French and Spanish and more like that of other American territories. However, for the Orleans Territory, two unique political organizations were created—the parish system and the police jury. Instead of counties, as in other territories, in 1807 Louisiana was divided into sections called parishes based on the Catholic parishes of its French and Spanish colonial periods. A judge, law enforcement officers, and a twelve-member council, known as a police jury, handled the government tasks in each parish.

By 1810, the Orleans Territory had about 76,000 people, more than the 60,000 required for statehood. In 1811, the U.S. Congress authorized the writing of a state constitution, which residents accomplished in 1812.

On April 30, 1812, the Orleans Territory of the Louisiana Purchase became the eighteenth state—named Louisiana. In June, residents elected William Claiborne as their first state governor. The remaining Louisiana Territory was renamed the Missouri Territory to avoid confusion with the new state.

Battle of New Orleans

Although Louisiana became a state in 1812, many people in the northern areas of the country still distrusted Louisiana residents because of their diverse mix of ethnic backgrounds. The turning point in the rest of the country's relationship with Louisiana residents came during the War of 1812 (1812–1815). Americans had declared war on Britain because Britain violated U.S. shipping rights and routinely captured and forced American sailors to work on their ships.

When British forces advanced on the city of New Orleans in December 1814, General Andrew Jackson defended the city

with troops. Jackson commanded one of the most diverse groups of soldiers in the United States, including pirates, the First and Second Battalions of Free Men of Color, Chocktaw warriors, and military units from Kentucky, Tennessee, Mississippi, and Louisiana. This series of battles ended with Britain's defeat on January 8, 1815.

The Battle of New Orleans was the last fight of the war and the greatest U.S. victory. It forced Britain to honor the peace Treaty of Ghent and recognize U.S. claims to the Louisiana Territory and Florida. Louisiana residents had proved their loyalty and shown they were willing to die for the United States. From that time forward, few doubted that they were true Americans.

▲ An 1860s painting of a naval fight during the Battle of New Orleans. Andrew Jackson felt sure that America's gunboats would stop the British from approaching New Orleans from the east, but the British easily defeated them.

43

The Louisiana Purchase settled the debate between expansionists and those people who felt the United States was already large enough. In an instant, the United States owned the most land, and the balance of power, in North America.

As the U.S. population grew and moved to the West, additional states were carved from the Missouri Territory. The states of Arkansas, Missouri, Iowa, Minnesota, North Dakota, South Dakota, Nebraska, Oklahoma, Kansas, Montana, Wyoming, and Colorado all contain some territory acquired in the Louisiana Purchase.

The Louisiana Purchase, on the other hand, forever changed the lives of the diverse groups of people who had been living there long before the U.S. settlers arrived. Until the Louisiana Purchase, black people, both slaves and free, had enjoyed more freedoms and opportunities under the Spanish system of government than under the initial U.S. rule. Native Americans lost their land because the U.S. government broke treaties and took it. The traditional lifestyles of various ethnic groups were attacked by Anglo settlers who believed in the superiority of their way of life and who harshly imposed U.S. government on them.

By allowing Louisiana statehood, however, Congress had granted citizenship to a mixture of people, thus slowly beginning the necessary process of accepting diversity into the Union. The legacy of the Louisiana Purchase was a new vision of the United States as a diverse, powerful country that stretched from coast to coast. The *National Register* exclaimed, "It is thus we stride, from object to object; and shall eventually light upon the banks of the river Columbia and the shores of the Pacific! What magnificent prospects open us!" The Louisiana Purchase convinced most Americans of their Manifest Destiny and created a feeling of pride, possibility, and nationalism in the developing United States.

1492: ▶ Columbus lands in the Americas and claims the land for Spain.

1682: ▶ René Robert Cavelier, sieur de La Salle, explores Mississippi River Valley and claims land for France. He names it the Louisiana Territory.

1698: ▶ King Louis XIV orders that colonies be formed in Louisiana Territory.

1718: ▶ New Orleans is founded along Mississippi River.

1722: ▶ New Orleans becomes the capital of Louisiana Territory.

1754: ▶ French and Indian War begins.

1762: ▶ France gives Louisiana Territory to Spain.

1763: ▶ Britain wins the French and Indian War.

1775: ▶ American Revolution begins.

1783: ▶ American Revolution ends, and the United States is formed.

1784: ▶ Spain closes Mississippi River to U.S. trade.

1789: ▶ French Revolution begins.

1795: ▶ The Treaty of San Lorenzo opens the Mississippi River to Americans.

1800: ▶ Napoleon regains Louisiana Territory from Spain.

1802: ▶ Napoleon fights to regain Saint-Domingue.

1803: ▶ The Louisiana Purchase doubles the size of the United States.

1804: ▶ Louisiana Purchase land is divided into Orleans Territory and District of Louisiana.

1812: ▶ The Orleans Territory joins the Union as the state of Louisiana.

1821: ▶ Mexico wins independence from Spain.

1830: ▶ Congress passes the Indian Removal Act, which legalizes the removal and resettlement of Native American groups.

1845: ▶ John O'Sullivan first uses term Manifest Destiny; Texas becomes a state.

1846: ▶ Mexican-American War begins.

1848: ▶ January 24—James Marshall finds gold at Sutter's Mill. February 2—Mexican-American War ends when Treaty of Guadalupe Hidalgo is signed.

1850: ▶ California becomes a state.

1861: ▶ Civil War begins.

1864: ▶ Nevada becomes a state.

1865: ▶ Civil War ends.

1867: ▶ United States buys Alaska from Russia.

1887: ▶ Native American traditional homelands are eliminated when Congress passes the Dawes Act.

1900: ▶ Hawaii becomes a U.S. territory.

1907: ▶ Oklahoma becomes a state.

1912: ▶ New Mexico and Arizona become states.

abolitionists: people who worked to outlaw slavery

ally: one that is united in alliance with another, especially by treaty

Anglo: person of non-Spanish, European descent

aristocratic: belonging to a hereditary ruling class, or nobility

buffer: something that separates potentially antagonistic entities, as an area between two rival powers that serves to lessen the danger of conflict

ceding: to surrender possession of, especially by treaty

coalition: an alliance, especially a temporary one, of people, factions, parties, or nations

diverse: consisting of distinct characteristics, qualities, or elements

economy: system of producing and distributing goods and services

empire: political power that controls large territory, usually consisting of colonies or other nations

guillotine: a device consisting of a heavy blade held aloft between upright guides and dropped to behead the victim below

indigo: any of various shrubs or herbs of the genus Indigofera in the pea family; also a blue dye obtained from these plants

manifest: obviously true and easily recognizable; the term Manifest Destiny meant that the true and obvious destiny of the United States was to expand its borders to the Pacific Ocean

monarchy: a state ruled or headed by a monarch, such as a king or queen

natural resources: naturally occurring minerals—such as oil and gold—that can be used or sold, or geographical features, such as a good harbor or climate

plantation: a large estate or farm on which crops are raised, often by slaves or resident workers

right of deposit: permission to unload goods at ports without paying fees to the ruling government

seaboard: coastal land near the sea

smuggler: someone who imports or exports without paying lawful customs charges or duties

steward: person who manages another's property, finances, or other affairs

territory: geographical area that belongs to and is governed by a country but is not included in any of its states

treaty: agreement made between two or more people or groups of people after negotiation, usually at the end of a period of conflict

Books

Alagna, Magdalena. *The Louisiana Purchase: Expanding America's Boundaries.* New York: Rosen, 2004.

Blumberg, Rhoda. *York's Adventures with Lewis and Clark: An African-American's Part in the Great Expedition.* New York: Harper Collins, 2004.

Carter, E. J. *The Lewis and Clark Journals.* Chicago: Heinemann, 2003.

DeKeyser, Stacy. *Sacagawea.* New York: Franklin Watts, 2004.

King, David. *American Voices: Westward Expansion.* New York: John Wiley & Sons, 2003.

Long, Cathryn J. *Westward Expansion.* San Diego: Kidhaven Press, 2003.

Pierce, Alan. *The Louisiana Purchase.* Edina, Minn.: Abdo Daughters, 2004.

Web Sites

Cabildo Online
http://lsm.crt.state.la.us/cabildo/cab 1.htm

Lewis and Clark Interpretive Center
http://www.fs.fed.us/r1/lewisclark/lcic/

Lewis and Clark Trail
http://lewisandclarktrail.com/legacy/ sold.htm

Monticello: The Home of Thomas Jefferson
http://www.monticello.org

Napoleon
http://www.napoleon.org/en/home.asp